I0211810

Look How Alive

⚭

poems by Lauren Hollingsworth-Smith

Write Bloody UK

www.writebloodyuk.co.uk

Copyright © Lauren Hollingsworth-Smith, 2022.

All rights reserved. No part of this book may be used, performed, or reproduced in any manner whatsoever without written permission from the publisher except in the case of brief quotations embodied in critical articles or reviews.

First edition.
ISBN: 978-1-8380332-5-5

Cover Design by Angelo Maneage
Interior Layout by Winona León
Edited by Fern Beattie and Vicky Morris
Proofread by Fern Beattie
Illustrations by Lauren Hollingsworth-Smith

Type set in Bergamo.

Write Bloody UK
London, UK

Support Independent Presses
writebloodyuk.co.uk

LOOK HOW ALIVE

LOOK HOW ALIVE

Part I

Part II

PART I

When one is alone and lonely, the body
gladly lingers in the wind or the rain,
or splashes into the cold river, or
pushes through the ice-crusted snow.
Anything that touches.

Mary Oliver

I Want to Stand Naked in the School Hall

on the podium, mid assembly,
so my presence will be so overbearing no one can look away.
I want their eyes to burn into my skin, examine
its ripples and folds and the scar that digs it up
like a trench in Ypres.

I'd watch a few hundred jaws slowly unhinge,
drop down into a mass of O's, all directed
at my body, lopsided like the projector, its flourescent beams
bouncing on my raw flesh so each goosebump
would have its own time in the spotlight.

I want to raise my arms, outstretch my fingertips,
so everyone can see my hairy armpits and wonky tits,
my nipples erect with the cold of a hundred stark looks,
so they'd know, so they'd see, I'm not perfect
and in no way do I want to be. Then,

when I've got their attention, I want to read them a poem
through the headteacher's microphone, full blast
so that each naked syllable in each naked word,
spat from my naked throat, would near burst their eardrums,
before they stood, frozen and agape, then filed out.

SPL

Dad reads *The Enchanted Wood*
to me and Mia in the big front room.
The log fire crackles and spits, casting
orange spirits on the wall.

We pick dandelions and elderberries
to make wine. The cellar is full of dusty
demijohns, the smell of damp stone.
It's scary, full of spiders.

Stepmum 1 makes us ragdolls from our old tights.
She called them *Mary-Jane* and *Trudy*.

Stepmum 1 went to the shops.
She never came back.

In the middle of eating Sunday dinner,
we have to go next door because an ambulance
is coming for Dad, and he doesn't want us to see.

He drops a plate on his arm,
Blood shoots out like the water jets at Clifton Park.
When we're cleaning up with Mamam, I think
the kitchen is splattered with ketchup.

IT

There are holes in our bedroom floorboards
like mouths. One ate my favourite *Puppy in my Pocket*.
I reach down my arm but can't get it back, so cry.
The Neighbours bang their *be quiet* on the walls.

We like curling up in the top airing cupboard,
owlets in a warm towel nest.

I'm   upside   down   over
the   viaduct   barrier
the ground so far away, the trees look smaller
than broccoli, mum's boyfriend's hands jiggle
my feet as if I'm Trudy. I'm scared he –
Mandy am gonna drop 'er! Am gonna drop 'er!

The limp body of our cat hangs
from the locked jaws of boyfriend 1's dog.

Summer smells like hot tarmac. We run barefoot
after the ice-cream van, eat 50p Mr Whippys
on the green fence, swaying our feet.

We climb up neighbourhood porch roofs,
ending flakes of white paint scattering
under our sandal soles.

Dad bounces us on springy heather
in the Peak District, the sky cracks open
and leaks yellow like a raw egg.

Kale juice in the morning.

We take yellow omega 3 tablets.

Spirulina, vitamin B, vitamin D.

Few suck on fruit mocktails with sparklers
and mini umbrellas in Greece, dance
on the bar table, the waiters give us
T-shirts but they're too big.

In the Blue Room dad puts a giant canvas on
the wall, and screws in a projector. It's like a
cinema. We play giant Mario kart.

Stepmum 2 throws shoes at us to say
Tidy your shit away.

Singing happy birthday feels awkward
because they have to fit *Dear Lauren, Mia
and Gowan* into it, and no one knows which
order to say the names in, or at what pace
to say them so the middle of the song
just turns into a jumble of noise.

Smiley faces and beans for tea.

I dip my happy meal chip in strawberry milkshake.

Mum takes citalopram.

We eat seaside donuts in Skeggy.

We have to go to the corner shop to buy gas
for tonight's bath and a Freddo each. I like running
my fingers across the grey box TV, feeling the static
crackle when it turns on. We put pound coins
in a box to watch it.

We're in debt but I don't understand what that means
even when we watch all the furniture slowly disappear
until there's just two beds and a sofa.

Boyfriend 2 slurs *goodnight tiger*
with beer breath. I hate the new house,
it smells weird.

For our fourteenth we have jelly shots
and play *Just Dance* with Holly.

We're helping Dad pick cabbage and chard
from the allotment. Earlier, Stepmum 2 threatened
to kick me out. I didn't see the blood I leaked
on the bathmat. Red is the colour of shame.

to Dad's

I'm filling in a form for my provisional license,
unsure which address to put down.

Hollingsworth

GCSEs are coming up. All my textbooks are kept
in a big Tesco carrier bag 'cos I have to keep moving
them from Mum's

to Mum's.

When I print my name in capital letters,
it's too long to fit on the line

Smith.

When I Fell in Love with My English Teacher

Half the class fancied her. Once, one of the lads
had an erection when she read out *Great Expectations*.

Like he said, *she was reyt fit*. In her wedding photos
I saw a *White Bindweed Fairy*. But for me

it was how she marked my stories and poems twice,
one comment checking *AQA Assessment Objectives*,

one for your craft as a writer. I'd stay after the last bell,
sometimes for hours, pick at my thumbs, splutter out

I'm not ready for exams or *I don't know what to do
with my life* and she'd sit with me and say *Oh Lordy,*

make a cup of tea, help me piece myself together.
I loved how she kept a jar of Nutella in the filing cabinet,

pronounced *genuine* like *gen-u-ein,* her stories of being
my age at school, playing hide-and-seek after dark,

scaring the shit out of friends. I even let her read
my diary once. In our last class, she illegally

smuggled Maccies breakfasts in for us and made
the whole corridor smell of sausage McMuffins and grease.

I remember sitting in the staffroom with her,
cutting up Shakespeare quotes for the display board,

our wrists accidentally brushed and for a second
I was a hive full of bees - tingling, buzzing.

PAINTING PEOPLE

is what I want to be doing. Spending hours
mixing flesh tones, to be reminded
that looking at skin is like looking
through that Pink Floyd prism, seeing it
separate into purple, yellow, green, marine.

I like big, bold, rough painting, slapping it on
like my brush is a boot caked in mud, my canvas
a wall, channelling last week's translation grade, too many
overdue essays, my constant bad hair days into screaming
mouths, slab-thrown faces of black and grey.

I like sculpting them in oils, their peanut-butter
thickness that stains my arms and hands
for days, their silt under my fingernails. I like noticing –
a line on a face, a wisp of baby hair,
how foreheads and cheeks are like moons

with their bumps and craters; the moisture on lips,
glossy pebble teeth. I like stroking paper with brushes
thin as eyelashes, smudging hues together
with my little finger, making shadows, blinking life
into eyes with a tiny white speck.

First Time, I

It was like a watercolour painting,
delicate, her lips coating me

in a soft cadmium, planting pigment
across my cheeks, down my neck,

and her hands, soft and light as the paws
of a butterfly, scuttled across the hills

of my body, hesitant at the crest,
asking for permission, and when granted,

peeled my shorts from my skin as if
my legs were made of hollow eggshells.

And I became a flower lifting up its head,
my petals unfolding gently, as we melted into

the scene on her bedcovers, a tableau of blossoms
and butterflies, I blooming, she drinking my nectar.

BACKWARDS

Sometimes I want to grow backwards,
for my back to open up like a mouth,
spit out chunks of metal, and my spine,
escaping its prison bars, to smile and curve in.

My ribs would wrap around my heart like a fist
squeezing the juice out of an orange.
My body trying to fold itself in half,
my rib bones grind against my hip bones,

my spine contorting itself like it's trapped in
a cupboard – then stop, and like a twisted
pea shoot reaching up to the sun,
straighten, straighten perfectly

and my shoulders would be completely aligned
for the second time, my sardine toes
spreading out like frog feet, so I could
draw smiley faces on them in biro.

The balls in my chest would deflate, the Saturn
rings around my nipples shrink and turn baby pink;
my limbs would thin and hollow out until
I'm as light and nimble as a blue tit

and my hair would would unwind into my scalp –
like ravelling up a ball of yarn until it's like soft tufts
of goose feathers grassing my skull,
and I'd spit out my teeth like they're little balls

of chewing gum, and my body would be
small enough to be nursed like a coffee cup.
It'd be acceptable for me to scream and cry
for love and attention and I'd keep shrinking,

gulping in screams like a figure drowning
until I swallow up the last howl
and I'm gone, have turned out the lights,
rolled myself up in womb-water duvets.

LITTLE BOY ON THE TRAIN

Thumb crooked on his lip,
wet and gnarled like rippled bark,
watching trees get sucked backwards.
He's making fish and ladybirds from rivulets of rain,
listening to the milk bottle rattle of the train.
Then he's swallowed up by a black tunnel mouth.

It's nighttime! It's nighttime!

His head drops to his shoulder,
on a puppet master's string,
eyelids squeeze cheeks, he snorts in
and whistles out, pretending
he's in the land of nod.
The tunnel spits him out in a flash of light.

Electric shock,
he bolts upright.

It's daytime again!

Reuben's Grin

We were playing cowboy shoot out,
and when the imaginary bullet hit his chest
he fell too fast and landed on his back.
His eyes widened and I saw crevices clench
across his cheeks as he strained against tears.

But he didn't cry. He just sat cross-legged
on the carpet, observing, and after a minute
staggered back up to join in. Shy, when
the others grouped up on tasks
he worked on his own, sat at the desk

in the corner, between the smart board
and the window, eyes wide like a rabbit
at the blank paper in front of him. I asked
if he needed help and he meekly commented
I'm not good at writing reviews.

He drew some slanted boxes, each bearing
a lopsided dog head, and wrote *Pick a Dog
is good because you get to pick cute dogs.*
I suggested he could illustrate the magazine cover.
He asked if we could play the board game he made

where he was *Fire Boy*, pulled out a piece of paper and dice
from his zip-lock plastic wallet. Shook it upside down
to let paper snippings fall out – our items,
and explained the rules, words tumbling out
so fast they all slurred together.

He rolled a six and hiked across a volcano,
acquiring a key. With my wand, as instructed
I put lava on him to make him drop it.
And when I mimicked its hot sizzle – *psssssst,*
Fire Boy's smile sparked a flame that lit the room.

CONFESSIONS

I stole a Freddo from the newsagents aged nine.
In comp I used to daydream about being kidnapped
by Miss Hunter, imagined sipping hot chocolates

in her kitchen, certain she'd have mugs with cats on.
I told my sister I was sleeping at Fran's but actually,
I met this girl from Tinder who had a girlfriend but

it was *complicated*. We smoked blunts until I woke
up being spoon-fed honey on a kitchen floor,
dregs of vomit in my hair like curdled milk.

During lockdown I went on a *long walk* to the woods,
met my girlfriend and fucked on a fallen tree.
Last year I went home in a drunk stranger's car boot.

When my kayak capsized and I couldn't find the pull
on my spraydeck, I didn't fight, I let my lungs fill
with river water like elastic bands about to snap.

Four Reasons My Ex Is Like This Canal

1, When I try to talk to her, she's still and quiet,
staring through me with glazed apathy,

sleek and poised. She's no river,
roaring like the wingbeat of a thousand starlings,

all fiery and alive and moving; she's just canal:
a static line of dead water.

2, I can't help finding beauty in her, still.
Empty beer cans glint like white waterlilies.

It's in the small things, her freckles of sunlight,
the orange flick of a salmon's tail,

the petrol skin of her body, how it offers
back light in small rainbows.

3, Every time I look at her, I see myself
staring back, until a slow-moving barge

ploughs through and our mirage
separates, so I remember us holidaying

on the broads, legs dangling
from a long boat roof, wind ruffling our hair,

water shimmying to the engine's hum, trees
leaning in to watch us kiss.

4, I'm drawn to her like midge fly, stuck
hovering, drunk on sweet damp musk.

I won't leave.
My body buzzes with longing.

The Five Stages

after Mary-Jean Chan

I

Denial

You're there in the mornings, a grass blade from my face, with flaky
dandruff lips parted so the half-moons of your teeth just poke out and
breath escapes in deep, careful drags. I reach out my hand to your hair
and there's only cold pillow. So I'll reread our letters, watch you grow
up through your handwriting. Thirteen, thick, bubbly cursive: *I think
I might be gay but I don't know,* eighteen, tall winding notes on our van
design: *oven has to go here because gas is under bed to the left.* I hold your words
like a stillborn.

II

Anger

I think of the two bodies you slept next to that weren't mine. A girl,
my childhood friend. A boy, your flatmate. You didn't like my sadness.
The way it spiralled into your life like a bird through an open window,
flapping, knocking over your rainbow ordered pen pots, screeching. I
smash a mug and it feels good so smash more, kick the porcelain snow-
mound on my carpet, tweeze out a white flake from my big toe. You love
tweezing things out – my eyebrow hairs, blackheads, the scar on my spine
– examining with pride the black peppercorns of dirt and yellow-white
worms before crumpling up the tissue.

III

Depression

My days stop being days. Like candle wax, they've merged into a
hardened puddle, the wick burnt down. I measure the passing of time
by the shrinking of my body. I can see each individual slat of my ribcage
now. I drift in and out of sleep. There are moments, just before waking,
where I forget the thing nesting in my chest. Then I plunge into the icy
pool of my consciousness, my body smacks against the water cold and
hard.

IV

Bargaining

I walk to the train station and imagine what it's like: the deafening
thunder claps, the squeal slicing through my ears, my innards covering
the tracks like squashed raspberries, and then –
nothing. I become a magpie, collecting the little things I can use: tablets,
blades, bottles of booze.

V

Acceptance

I'm alone in the middle of a mountain valley. The wind running,
glistening white on the long grasses, the purple orchids twisting flamenco.
The whistle of a marmot bounces from one snow-capped peak to the
other; crickets leap in and out of my pool of vision in brown specs. And
the ground is endless. Straw-coloured grass and leaning crags stretch out
until they meet the clouds. I empty my lungs and the sky and dirt and
rockfaces throw my voice back at me: *I'm alone. I'm alive.*

Emails

Absences and missed work
Dear Lauren,
I hope this finds you well. A couple of tutors have alerted me to the fact
that you have missed classes and failed to submit work for them –
and what is more, that you did not notify the tutors in advance.

RE: chat
It was good to see you just now Lauren. As I said on our call
I recommend you use the university's counselling service – here's the link to register

5th week blues?
Dear tutees, 5th week is upon us, along with the challenge of a new lockdown
This is guaranteed to boost flagging spirits [video of a small dog in a panda costume]

Psychoeducational resources
[attachment]
We have all heard people say "You need to be more assertive!"
But what exactly is assertiveness? Assertiveness is a communication style.
It is being able to express your feelings in an open manner that doesn't
violate the rights of others

RE: Commentary extension
I'm deeply shocked to hear this, and hope that your respiratory problems have now
subsided. Please do let me know if you'd like the opportunity to chat with me some
more about this, or if there is anything I can do to be of support to you.

Prose work
fwd.
More work is required in order to make progress, with texts showing errors in the
choice of tenses, the form of negations and pronouns, and generally little attention to
orthographic detail.

RE: checking in
Thanks for your email. I'm glad you are back in college but sorry to hear you are
still not feeling well.
I'm available to talk if you'd like to speak about the incident, since I was there.

Psychoeducational resources
[attachment]
Myth 3: "If I am assertive I have to be assertive in every situation"

RE: teams meeting
Dear Lauren,
It is good of you to write. I was aware that you had been in hospital and I have been thinking of you with concern and sending good thoughts and wishes.

Checking in
Dear Lauren
I hope the journey home went well and that you are settling back in. I know that being at home isn't what you wanted and I am happy to chat with you about this.

RE: medical letter
It is disappointing and of some concern that you did not register or see your local GP until August. You were removed from college in May.

Dog

My chest is a flock of seagulls stuck
in an oil spill, screeching uncontrollably,

their feathers soaked in thick blackness,
wings like weights. The dog bites down

like the sound of a fork scraping a glass bowl,
but the sound doesn't end, it keeps scraping.

The dog eats the gulls. Their bones crackle
like sweet wrappers. The crisis team are saying

What do you want?
          I don't want to exist.

That's not the same as wanting to die.
               I don't want to exist.

Lauren that's not possible.
                    I don't want to exist.

Lauren how can we help you?
                    I don't want to exist.

*Lauren [sound of forks
scraping bowls]*

A TOUCH OF THE BLUES.
An erasure, *Daily Mail*, 14th October 2009

█████████████ Mr Ddungu had been ██████ to a meeting with his tutors as he ███ failed to complete an assignment.

They thought he had a 'touch of the blues' █████████████████████ ████████████████████

Professor █████████████ said: 'I wouldn't say he had a serious problem. ████████████████████████ John█

██said: 'I'm feeling ███████ down and ████████ under pressure.'

Prof██ ████████████████████ was 'very surprised' by the death, █████████ 'In my mind, ████████████████ he had the blues. I'd heard this before ███████████

Mr Ddungu ████████████████████████ ██████████████████

██ took his life ████████████████████

██ ████████████████████

████████████████████████

Mr Ddungu's mother████████████████████████████████ was too upset to comment. ████████

PART II

BLUEBIRD CAFÉ

Nestled on a cobbled side street in Portobello
with mint green table sets scattered outside

and the sun hitting my face like a shower head,
Nina Cassian's poems bathing on the metal warmth,

I finish the first full meal I've had in two months.
After paying, the waiter hands me a paper bag,

grinning. Inside is a chocolate tart, heart-shaped.
It's almost as if he knew.

ADVICE
for Mam'am

Stick to your guns, girls
and don't you quit.

If anyone gives you stick
tell 'em, taters!
Stick to you guns girls

when you go down there.
Don't listen to the pompous sods
and don't you quit.

Full-time carer for two
and *garden horse*
stick to your guns,

think of our poem, hung
on't fridge – *rest if you must,*
but don't you quit,

Mam'am, mowin t'lawn
with a broken wrist
Stick to your guns, and don't you quit.

SEAGULL

You do not know grace, stumbling through the air
like a drunkard. Your call is thick and rasping – post-pub
brawl slurring in the car park, a gargling cough syrup cry.

Spasming bird, convulsing your neck, widening your beak,
guzzling day-old chips, ice cream, pink foam dribbling
from your mouth like rabies. You're a peasant, you'll never

belong in the azure seas of the Maldives with the finer birds –
it's the muddy slosh of Blackpool waves for you. And you'll never
be regal like the swan, its neck a calligrapher's question mark.

You know nothing of manners or etiquette,
only the scuffle of squabbling over scraps, your wings
double bent, metal screeching. Ugly bird

with piss-coloured eyes, pinhead blacks, the world's
biggest cold sore bulging on your beak. And yet, there is
a pride in your scruffiness, the way you strut,

your squawk rolling out with an opera singer's gusto.
Loud, unapologetic. You do not know grace.
And God, how I envy that you'll never want it.

TRAMLINES

A tidal wave of bodies
   jostling, jumping, skin clanging
        together sticky with sweat
and beer, hands like stalks
in a thunderstorm,
    sound spilling from a thousand of
  mouths thrown open in chorus,
the air thick and full
   with ground dust, smoke
     and strobe lights, I climb
       onto my sister's shoulders, look across
it all, stretching wide and out – this sea
    bursting with noise and colour. I let go
      and I am carried
     up, up, up. Surfing
         an ocean of hands
     my body bobbling with the
       clamour and sway of the tide
     free-flowing as music.

Cutting It Off

Are you sure sweetheart? It's a lot. I nod, my ears drink in
the gentle bee hum of the clippers, the sound tickles
the nape of my neck, then I feel it, the weight

lifting, the heavy absence. The strands fall supple
and soundless as fish slipping through a lake.
They carpet the tiles, soft. The barber scales

my head like a sculptor chiselling his marble bust,
hands contouring the ears and jaw, sand falling
to reveal the cranium, smooth and round as a bowl.

Then, the cricket-chirp of scissors begin
their slow rhythmic chorus. My hair floats away
from me like autumn leaves, big tufts

of mouse brown and blonde pile up.
I stare at its messy thatch. The parts of me
scattered, the dead girl on the floor.

Tableaux Parisiennes

It's half three in the morning and I'm speeding
down the city streets on an electric scooter,

cars passing in streaky red lines, the wind lashing
my cheeks like a cold bedsheet.

My hair is flying. I'm flying.
And even at this hour, the city is bubbling,

overspilling with lights that wobble
against the dark the way a lake carries stars,

and the air pulses, elastic with disco
carried from Pont Alexandre. An accordion

top notes the subway; clusters of revellers
smoke and twist to reggae on the grass,

and I'm streaming down the cobbles,
the traffic, the paint-stroked buildings,

Van Gogh café terraces, Matisse shop
windows, a streak of laughter.

How to Become Bilingual

Naturally, learn all the swear words first,
your boss exclaiming *Oh Putain!* as her daughter knocks
a ceramic bowl filled with caramel off the counter, scattering
white flakes like a snow-ball dispersing in slow motion,
gloopy bronze streaks making the black tile a marble temple floor.

Master the domestic — know your *torchons* from your *serviettes*,
go to the *machine à laver* five times a day, always dry the laundry
with the *étendroir* and never the *sèche-linge*, making sure blouses
are on a *cenitre*. Become best friends with the *aspirateur sans fil*
and the *lave-vaiselle*. do a *vite coup d'aspi* for waffle crumbs

from the kids' *goûter*, a *coup de chiffonnette* for any spillages.
If the hoover has run out of battery, use the *balai,*
and the *balainette* for broken shards of firewood, pine-needles.
Go on dates with random French men even though
you don't think you're attracted to their gender.

Tell yourself this isn't morally wrong, you're just finding yourself,
and after enough beers anyone's skin feels warm
and safe to lie next to. Still, wish it was her skin and spend
nights burying your wet eyes at the cold edges of pillows.
Take on a new identity. You are no longer *Lauren*

but *Laurènne*, stress on the last syllable; an iamb now,
a heartbeat. You are *Nou-Nou, Lolo* at work
and *blue-hair-girl* in bars. Realise you should tone-down
the drinking when a face you've never seen smiles
and hugs you, saying *nous nous sommes rencontrés l'autre nuit au Moose,*

get shitfaced anyway and think fuck it, *I'm a poet,*
we're all depressed alcoholics – a radio host once said this to you
in an email so you know it's true. Wonder why everything here
is made of *pâte*: *pâte à crèpe*, pancake batter, *pâte polymère*,
modelling clay, *pâte à tartiner*, chocolate spread,

pâte à mâcher, chewing gum, *pâte à proute*, farting putty.
Start getting free stuff from French people because you can
speak French – a brown leather belt from the boutique owner
who tells you *ça va aller parfait avec ce jean* and starts saving you
new clothes behind the counter, *c'est vraiment votre style*.

Two euros off your coffee because *tu parles*
très bien francais. Fall in love with the poetry of
the language: you're annoying me is *tu me gonfle*,
you're inflating me. Unrequited love is
la douleur exquise –the exquisite pain.

THE FOG

I've never seen anything like it –
September morning, seven thirty, the day fresh,
sun newly risen, white gold, air a leaf of iceberg lettuce,
and the sky clean as a kitten's yawn, frost blue.

On the other side of the fence there it is,
a gushing river of cloud, eddying around the mountain rocks,
tumbling white like seafoam, thicker and softer
than my sherpa dressing gown cuffs that hang down

as I watch it mock the faint, warm plumes of my breath,
the steam from my tea mug dissipating in washed out grey,
puny in comparison to this swirling stampede
of white horses. White Vesuvius, smothering all.

Poem About a French Guy Who Danced with Me

in Loop Bar, Tignes – to some electro club beat,
our bodies bumping and twisting together.
The next day he swung open his van door,
paper bag and skateboard in hand, plonked

down warm bread and croissants, simply
bellowing *Baguette!* with a smile.
For a while we sat there, under the soft
weight of the morning, jazz oozing

from his laptop like treacle, the air coffee-scented,
my hands leafing the pages of my book
between mouthfuls of pastry. His head

on my shoulder, breaths lengthening
back towards slumber. And, knowing
we were strangers, I fell asleep too.

THE MOON STRIPPING

is no frivolous matter.
She takes time and care,
gently unpeeling her layers
like the papery skins of a garlic.
She reveals herself in lunar segments,
pulls down the shadows on her lacy skirt
so it hangs just below her mascon bone, exposing
a slither of crescent-cut flesh. Then flashes a grin, noticing
the tide leaning in to kiss her dusty cheek. You want to slip off
her navy drawers and skinny dip the darkness with her, Lady Godiva,
bathing the world in her nudity, laughing luna because you can only watch.

La Vallée Perdue

In the morning, you showed me the route,
your hand tracing the contour lines as if
caressing the wrinkled cheek of a grandfather.

On the trail, the sky was so blue and clear
it could have been one sweeping block of
acrylic paint. The ground buzzed alive,
wildflowers splashed reds and blues

on the yellow-green like Holi powder.
A herd of semi-wild horses turned their
long necks towards us, then bowed their heads,
ears flicking hello, tongues grazing the rocks.

We wandered down sandy paths that
crackled like Velcro under our feet,
into the valley - French Arizona.
We crossed shingle rivers on long wood planks,

found a small cave where sun spots flitted
over the rocks like white moths, circled
up a crag edge with just blue frayed rope
to stop us from slipping. The mountains turned

into pines. I joked about being in a Ghibli movie
You yelled *Ashitaka!* and ran through the forest
to where you'd found a wooden sign
planted in the dirt with BAR → 50M

written in shaky red paint. And sure enough,
up the dirt track there stood a log building
where we soon lay on balcony deckchairs
sipping beers, you tasting your first hotdog.

And I thought it crazy how you'd made it
to twenty-, maybe thirty-something, having
never had one, how I was here, with some
French man I met in a nightclub, and how

the Lac de Chevril was clearer and bluer
than a swimming pool; The hugeness
of *Le Voile de la Mariée*, that rock giant,
her white ribbons streaming from the sky,

how we climbed her, swam in the pool
of her crown, before you left, and I watched
your van-home shrink into a white spot.

Homo

When I was six a boy kept chasing me and my sister
around the play area and hitting us, hissing *lesbians!*

I knew it was a nasty word by the way he spat it
out of his mouth like a fish bone.

When I told mum that he kept calling us lesbians
her boyfriend laughed.

My boss tells me, I *don't have a problem with it but please
don't tell my kids, I don't want them to know. If they ask you, pretend you have a boyfriend.*

My boss' son whispers *t'es homosexuelle* to wind up his sister.
She sniggers at the gay little mouse in her storybook.

People say *he sounds like a dick* when I talk about my ex.
They go *oh* and pause, looking uncomfortable when I say *he* was a *she.*

I've stopped correcting people.
What does it matter if they think she was a boy, she's gone now.

But still I think about the way she never let me wear dresses
because she didn't want to look like the gay one.

How she said it didn't mean anything when I called her beautiful
because I'm not a man and only men mean it when they say it.

How I'd wish I was a man.
My Tinder tells me:

we can't find anyone who fits your preferences right now but check back soon for new people.
Last night I dreamt I was in a nightclub and men kept touching me –

hands gripped my hips forcing me into a dance,
facial hair grazed my cheek like an abrasive sponge,

I felt the weight of a leg against my leg, fat hairy fingers on my thigh,
a voice saying *ça va ma jolie?*

And I screamed
I AM A LESBIAN

and the music stopped,
the crowd froze like a paused TV soap

before slowly turning towards me,
Va t'en. Get Out.

DUNNOCK

While the Robin pouts and puffs out his chest,
bright plumage ripe for Instagram, and the Wren struts,
throws back her head, bursts into a rendition of 'Halo' –
the Dunnock tuts and takes a drag from his cig.

His flat cap bobbing up and down as he shuffle-hops the ground,
and squeaks out a few wobbly notes of corrugated iron:
'Ey up Steve, fancy a pint int' Red Lion? Then he hauls himself
into the air, brown parka flapping in the wind.

He's the vanilla ice cream of birds, lowest in the pecking order.
A nice chap, but drab, spends his days in the scrub, minding his own,
shuffling about with that awkward gait. And he's meant to be chuffed
when the priest says – he's a model proletariat, seen but not heard.

What he means is a working-class bird. Out there in the bushes,
with four other dunnocks, all jumping like crickets, arses in the air,
tails proper waggling, doing it in true Rocky Horror fashion.
He winks, that Jack the Lad, chirps out a friendly fuck you –
I am the dunnock and I like to screw.

*Note: In the Victorian era the Dunnock was often used as a model for how the
working class should conduct themselves because of its dull, quiet and conservative
nature. It was later discovered that the Dunnock is polyamorous and often several
males and females will mate together.*

ROMANCE
after Nina Cassian

Forgive me for making you weep
I should have murdered you
I should have dragged out your soul
and battered you with it.

I should have plucked your rib
bones one by one and eaten them
Savoured the sound of their crunch
like salt and vinegar crisps.

I should have fed your lungs to the flies,
giggled at the tickle of a thousand mouths,
licking your sticky jam blood off my fingers.
I should have murdered you.

*lines in italic taken from Romance, Nina Cassian, Translated from Romanian by
Fleur Adcock

First Time, II

The bar is dim and glowing orange like at my dad's house
when we had the log fire on and the lights off,
and the walls wobbled and danced.

There's a man talking to me but I can't remember what he's saying
because time is slipping away before I can catch it.

He buys me a gin and tonic;
it sits heavy on my tongue.

*

There's a low jagged moan of metal against tile;
two single beds are pushed together.

I wonder how I ended up here

the man is kissing me and my clothes have disappeared

then it happens and I think

Oh, this is happening

*

I feel last night in my mouth, a thick blanket on my teeth.

A stranger's body presses next to mine
and stirs into consciousness.
Its limbs twitch out of sleep.
The breath lightens.

An arm coils around my back.
Fingers run through my hair.

He whispers   *t'es belle*
I feel the dew of his lips on my forehead
                tu as beaux cheveux
my nose
                belle nez
my mouth
                beaux lèvres

★

it happens again but this time I'm aware and I think

        Oh, this is what it's like.

I'm a cave on a beach,
And the sea is lurching, claw-shaped.

CHAMOIS

strung up by its horns on the garage roof
so newly dead it's almost living.
Its black nose glistens wet.
Its ears prick up tall
like the crack of the gunshot is still

bouncing through them.
There's almost a fire flickering in its eyes –
wide ovals of umber with flecks of yellow
and scarlet orbiting the black disc
which still seem to be looking,

drinking in the ceiling tube light.
Its fur is fresh coffee.
I want to touch the tufts of white
on its chest, feel the softness.
It's perfect.

The legs stretch down,
straight, trotters pointed with the grace
of a ballet dancer. Its head doesn't droop
but looks up, away from the gash
on its stomach where its furry skin hangs

open and loose like a Build-A-Bear
waiting to be stuffed. The flesh and bowels
scooped out, leaving a deep red cave,
blood dripping into the drain
like droplets from a stalactite.

MERITOCRACY

Last night I dreamed you tried to have sex with me
and it reminded me of when we were eleven and you stuck
your eel tongue down my throat and it writhed around,
poking at my cheek flesh and teeth. We'd both been chewing
gum and still had bits of it in our mouths floating

around our saliva pools like slithers of food
in a washing up bowl. And I wanted to tell you to stop
but I couldn't because your tongue was in my mouth.
Which makes me think of all the other girls you stuck
your tongue inside, how you'd pour vodka down them

until their legs caved and they lay, glass-eyed and still
like your sister's dolls and you'd tear through them
as if their bodies were grapes. I remember how their stories
were less important than your stories – a skimmed over typo,
a loose thread on your sub fusc, because you worked

so hard for your straight A*s. You had accolades for having
the most accolades. You even managed royal recognition
for e-safety whilst your grey-pink veiny dick stood waiting
on our phone screens. But that didn't matter. The stellar chemist,
our pride and joy, Wath's very own Oxford boy,

the world is yours, they'd say. *And you deserve it.*

PEOPLE I'VE KISSED

My best friend.
The first time was in her bedroom,
Awkward, clumsy. Her eyes flitting
from my eyes to my lips to my eyes to my lips.
For weeks after I'd doodle the shape of her mouth
in the margins of my Maths book,
the long, peach-fuzzed ridge under her nose,
her lower lip, curved and thick like the underside of
a spoon. Greek terraced houses teeth.

Five years later,
the girl in the *Plush* smoking area
who touched my arm a lot and called me cute.
It was soft and wet.
Friends said *it looked wholesome.*

The girl I was dancing with at the gay club
in Sheffield. After, she said
you're really fun, but I can't look after you,
where are your friends?

The French man who I think I could
have loved if he didn't disappear.

The French man who would later try to
fuck me while I was sleeping.

32-year-old Mitch from Sheff *(small world, 'ey)*
Who handed me a vodka and coke,
happy birthday. I had no interest in him
but I liked feeling desired,
the way he looked at me
glazed eyes holding my face, unmoving
                         -what?

-nothing love, absolutely nothing

The French girl who brushed her hands
across my jaw, my cheekbone, my skin follicles lifting
up like plant heads under her touch
You're so beautiful, seriously I love your face structure.
You make me want to cut my hair short.

The Dutch man wearing a knitted beige cardigan in a nightclub
watching whilst I was shaking hips on the box with the Pignatta staff,
shooting flügel, sliding down cage bars with my flatmate,
doing the worm in the middle of a circle, going outside,

Is it really blunt if I say I want to make out with you right now?

Oh. Sorry

Wow I would have never thought that. You don't look gay.

But how do you know you are if you've never had an experience with a man?

        [elbow knocks plastic pint cup to the floor]

Ha, now you owe me.

How was it? Was it bad?

'I don't see what women see in other women,' I'd told Doctor Nolan in my interview that noon. 'What does a woman see in a woman that she can't see in a man?'

Doctor Nolan paused. Then she said, 'Tenderness.'

That shut me up

Sylvia Plath, *The Bell Jar*

HER GHOST

Sometimes I talk to her. On alpine hikes
with jagged crags basking orange in the sun

and butterflies zipping in and out of my eyeline
in flashes of colour I turn and say –

you would have loved this, show her the painting
she made me, two women walking in the mountains.

Smoothing out the creases in my blue jumper
like icing a cake, I glance up *look how good I am*

at folding now. Her face is too washed out to reply
but I like to think she's smiling. Like all ghosts,

she likes to shapeshift.
Sometimes she's fourteen again, eyes laced in black

too thick to carry off, tossing her strawberry hair back,
her arms flailing, legs bouncing, heels twisting,

All Time Low blaring from her bedroom speaker
and laughter escaping her lips like a flurry of sparrows.

Or she's nineteen and we're together in her
dorm shower, my hips grin and melt

into warm dough from the soft grip of her hands.
Often, she turns into the girl, not the woman. Her body

straight and twig-like, her teeth wild.
We're backstage in the school play, dancing

a clumsy waltz to the lead out front. And somehow,
during the interval, our heads fall together

like two halves of a chopped lemon. Or we're sitting
on a damp fallen tree in the woods, silent,

watching the plumes of our breath mushroom out
as leaves fall like feathers. Like caterpillars probing,

our hands edge together – first the bump of little fingers,
then thumbs, then palm to palm, a cocoon of warmth,

then she claws me open with her razor nails,
and I'm gutted like a goat carcass, my jelly entrails

tumbling, squelching underfoot, until she sucks up
my small intestine like a strawberry lace.

Calmly, sternly, like a headteacher, she's saying *Go*
and my body collapses into string, I'm trying

to gather it up, roll it into a foetal position.
Go a bag of my t shirts and books lands at my feet.

She follows me into bars,
laughs at me when I'm kissing strangers –

I'm softer, I'm better. She likes to tease me still
step out of my forehead, smile and say, *okay,*

*I'll leave you in peace now, s*pread out her arms
and get swept up by the wind,

vanish into a wisp of a cloud on the skyline.
But she always comes back.

#NOTALLMEN
after Kim Moore

But the one who stuck his tongue
down my throat when I was eleven
and always had his hands on me.
The one who stole my body, too full
of rum mixers to say yes, to say no,
to even know what was going on.
The one who went past on his bike
then turned around, tailing me until
I banged fists on the hotel reception window.
The one who reached out a hand
from behind me, and cupped my breasts
whilst I ordered a drink, vanishing
when I turned. The one who took me,
falling asleep on his sofa after fajitas
with friends, as a permission slip,
who woke me trying to enter me.
Who couldn't understand stop
in five languages − *Arrête, stop,*
détengase, [shaking head] [recoiling]

Intersaison

When September comes, restaurant terraces stack up
their chairs, turn their signs to *fermé*, shops stop
lifting their shutters, buses stop purring down the roads.

The village centre becomes a graveyard of empty buildings –
only your footfalls clacking cobbles to break the headstone
silence. To buy bread and milk, you stand on the roadside

stick my thumb out, listening for a rumble breaking the empty,
sit on passenger seats next to strangers, the radio humming,
talking of au-pairing, Oxford, Sheffield. Green larches

put on angel halos, grey-brown rocky peaks are dusted with
icing sugar. The greens turn lemon. Spinachy needles
litter roads. Red and orange sweep over the mountains

like carnival ribbons. Fireweeds burn scarlet, send ash flakes
floating in the air. The valleys parade into their deaths,
flaunting gold, violet, carrot, umber, before the snow comes.

A Brief Encounter

I feel the forest move –
a flick of colour just outside my eyeline.
I turn and look. The fox stops and our
joint gaze binds us together in stillness.

He is no city fox.
The most he's seen of us is a tiny cluster
of streetlight stars, a small carpark perhaps.
Nothing more. He is hunter, not scavenger,
holds his body like a wolf.

Teeth hang past his mouth like icicles.
and his coat isn't traffic light orange
but sandy grey, like the rocks that watch
us watch each other. I slowly
reach for my camera. Fool

to crack the frozen air.

WHEN I FEEL LONELY, I SWIM

a slow breaststroke, so I can savour the water's touch
lapping up my tailbone to my neck, and back down.
Soft strokes in rhythm with the flip of my thighs

In

her warm body moves up my navel,
feather-brushes my breasts.

Out

She moves down my chest
to my calves, plants a hundred kisses
on my fingers and toes, rippling as she giggles

I take a long, deep breath
then plunge into her.

REMINDERS

There are moments, walking the light grey linoleum
of *Carrefour*, when my eyes fall on your toothpaste,
nestled on the shelf, plastic wrap glinting
from the white tube light, and my chest falls open
the way a banana peel drops down into a flower.
I think of my old toothbrush stood in its little family
on the windowsill, in my home that isn't my home anymore.
Green, the bristles frayed and bent backwards
like windswept birch trees, kept for too long
but it was a gift, it said, *you're welcome here, you're loved here.*
It's probably laying in some landfill heap now.
I remember when you half-carried me through
the bathroom door when I was too drunk to control
my limbs, my head lolling in circles, too heavy to hold up.
You propped me down on the toilet lid and brushed
my teeth for me. God, how I want to go back to that
old intimacy, brushing teeth, wiping each other's
snot with our sleeves. How it rendered me dizzy and alive.

That's over, but I can't help seeing kid-you
in the ten-year-old I nanny: the freckles scattered
across her nose, how her crayons must be put away
in rainbow order, how she measures each scissor-cut
of her paper snowflake to the exact millimetre,
so it's perfectly symmetrical. Her hands are like your hands –
nimble, precise always busy, fiddling with hair bobbles
or pens. Like you did, she only gets told off for singing
and dancing around the house too loud. I wonder
how many hours we spent loading the dishwasher,
you twirling around and singing after each plate was scraped.
She spends hours lost inside her headphones,
the music bubbling behind her eyelids, splattering
from her tapping feet, tumbling over her lips.

I had to stop myself from crying today, when
she swung her arms around and hurled out *Stone Cold*
by Demi Lovato. All I could see was us at the tram stop
in January swathed in the dark cold air, you changing
the chorus to *cold nose, cold nose,* laughing, shivering,
pressing your face into my chest for warmth.

Learning to Ski

think how the fuck can people control themselves with these
plastic landing strip feet, slipping down a hill and onto your arse,
legs tangled, falling back down every time you try stand like a toddler

> propel yourself across the flat with a ski on your left foot
> and nothing on your right, like riding a scooter. Watch an
> eleven-year-old bomb down a mountain and into a backflip.

At least now, you've perfected the *chasse-neige* and wide *virages,*
slowly snaking around the baby slope with triangle feet.
Then faster, weaving in between plastic cones,

> ski on one leg to learn how to turn sharply – *il faut cent pour cent*
> *de tes poids sur la jambe qui tourne !* Take your first chairlift.
> Become suddenly aware of the pull of gravity as you are dragged

hurtling towards earth from the heights of your first blue.
Master the art of falling: spread-eagle, legs in a knotted V,
sliding down on your belly like a penguin, tumbling sideways,

airborne for a brief eternity – arms out in front of you, legs up,
your body horizontal, really flying, before your goggles hit
and the stinging white clouds your vision. Fall in love with the thud

> and scatter, how it's like the perfect rippled plop of a pebble in water.
> Tame the wild horses you're buckled to. Knees bent,
> weight on the balls of your feet, shoulders facing forward.

Scream out loud *Yes!* after zig-zagging a steep narrow stretch
you had to bum-slide three days ago. Someone behind shouts
Wheyy! as you jump over a mogul and your face cracks into a moon.

> Start going really, really fast. *Tout schuss* down a red *peinte*, blasting
> fountains of white smoke behind you, pole strings flapping,
> the ground echoing your turns in its scraping hum.

> > Venture off-piste and feel what it's like to be weightless
> > as you float over waist-high powder, fall backwards
> > into its cloud cushion. And now, you don't have to think

about your movements. It's like dancing, grooving to the syncopated rhythm of the slope – the rises and sudden drops, big bumps, small bumps. Realise you are a dancer now, tangoing into a double helix.

Somehow, you've found yourself speeding down
the Grande Motte glacier, Italy unfolding into a frozen sea below
your eyeline, white storm waves lurching all the way to the blue glow of the sky.

LOVE POEM TO MYSELF
after Jack Underwood and Cia Mangat

Your hair after showering is my favourite thing. It's like the fluff
of fireweed seeds that float through the autumn air, like snow in reverse.

I love running my fingers through the soft fuzz of your undercut
which is long overdue a trim. But I like that you carry an unkemptness,

a certain wildness. Look at your hands, the bark gnarled and cracked,
the red craters from where you dug out your thumbs. They are artist's hands

with black threads under the fingernails – you always have with you
some trace of ink or paint or dirt. I love the dark stiff grass

on your calves, the white lace on your thighs, the small cluster above
your ankle, always missed when you shave. Your jawline demands

to be seen: cutting down past your ear, clean and sharp
as the crag edges on Col de la Fresse. You hold your early wrinkles

the way mountains hold thunderstorms in their crimps,
Time sprawling across the rockface in black neuron lines.

I love the way you feel things: how when you're sad you let it hit you
like a tsunami wave crashing over a wood beach hut –

splinters flying up and out like wooden fireworks;
white jaws gnashing and spitting, all pushed under the endless black.

And when you're happy it swells up inside your chest
and grows and grows until you're consumed by it, hot air

cursing through your toes, up your spine,
across your cheekbones, melting all but the now.

SUNRISE RIDE

At five in the morning, I pull open the door,
heave my body into the endless black mouth
that glitters. I've never seen the sky so naked,
than here, *Les Boisses*, tiny mountain hamlet
surrounded by the endless pines and mountains,

the silence that hangs heavy in the air
like a raincloud. Stiller than a rock.
The winding paths are the only things
that are not black. Snow refuses darkness.
It squeaks like rubber under my boots

as I climb the piste with my toe caps,
kicking a ledge into the peinte
then pushing down, following the pole
silouhettes, reverse runway lights.
A star falls. Its white tail flashes.

The top of the gondola, that familiar rectangle
is rising, a shadow against the dark slate sky
with its white sand grains. Here's the picnic bench.
Behind the peak of Tovière the sun lifts its head,
white like a moon, then yellowy

ink blots of orange, pink, blue bleed into each other,
colour spills over the mountain, trees yawn
into their greenness. I click into my skis
then slip down the clean, fork grooved white,
smooth as glass, moving like water.

It's Okay to Break
after Nikita Gill and Clarissa Pinkola Estés

Everything does: trees grow tired and give up,
drop their heavy boughs and watch the weight
they strained against shrivel up into confetti.

Clouds lurch, moan and split apart, let the rain
fall through. The earth is broken up by rivers –
chiselled and beaten into V-shaped valleys,

spurs like the jags on a zip. Cliffs are broken
and hollowed out into caves. Waves break
and they're beautiful. Their slow, emphatic

headbang. The white fireworks, the bellow
and hiss, have captivated artists for centuries.
The world is made of breaking, growing things:

buds sprout from naked branches, seeds break
to let out green shoots, the sky breaks
to let in the sun. *La Loba gathers up broken pieces,*

discarded entrails, and sings life into them:
and that is when the rib bones and leg bones begin
to flesh out, and the creature becomes furred.

La Loba sings some more and more of the creature
comes into being; its tail curls upward, shaggy and strong.
And still La Loba sings so deeply that the floor

of the desert shakes, and as she sings, the wolf
opens its eyes, leaps up, and runs away
down the canyon. Somewhere in its running,

whether by the speed or by splashing its
way into a river, or by a ray of sunlight
or moonlight hitting it right in its side,

the wolf is suddenly transformed into
a laughing woman who runs free towards
the horizon. And you, you are made up

of the same things that make up the waves
and the valleys, the trees, the dismantled skeleton
in the desert waiting to be found.

So break down, fall apart, crumble.
Let the shoots push through.
Let the wolf leap out.

Note: Lines in italic are taken from Women Who Run with the Wolves *by Clarissa Pinkola Estes*

LAURÈNNE

wears tight leather jeans and a crop-top
that could pass for a bra, *Wild Cherry* lipstick

and *Better Than Sex* mascara. Waiters wink
and place Génépy shots at her table,

free of charge, men at bars flash their cards,
what would you like?

She takes her pornstar martini
and disappears into the night.

Laurènne moves like a cobra, hips curling, leathery hide
flashing in the strobe lights. She is pole-dancing

to whistles and howls, taking bows from a spinning shaft.
She steps out of discotheque smoke like Venus rising

from frothy sea spume. She is neon electropop
vibrating like a jackhammer, she is a sticky underground

dancefloor, she is lifting up and onto a stage to fall back
into a hundred electric hands.

Rachele

We don't call or text much,
your voice is too fluid
to be contained in screens.
Instead, we send, long,
rambling audio notes and I cup
your voice in my hands like water,
let you trickle through
the cracks of my fingers
Hey sweetheart
Today I woked up, I woke up at five am...

Rachele, we met on your birthday
Mid-February. This makes you
an Aquarius: water-bearer, air sign.
So the snow was no coincidence.
Nor the way you danced so messy
and yelled *BURRATA* at the restaurant.
You're a true aquarian: *loud,* strong.
Our boss' fancy coffee machine was
too American, too watery for you
so every morning you'd brew us
real caffè Italiano in your stovetop moka pot.

Our time together was like those
espressos – short, fierce.
Jumping over the turnstile barriers
to smuggle onto the funicular
to the Grande Motte peak,
nights after work getting stoned
off our faces in your bedroom,
exchanging life stories under candlelight
and incense smoke. The time we
club-hopped until we were stranded at 3am

so hiked up a hill caked in snow and ice
in heels and slept in the *Bollin* staffroom.
It was tender too. Your soft fingers,
circling a clay mask under my eyes,
our bodies sprawled across the
sauna benches, heavy with calmness,
you talking about your German summers,
your complicated family, bike rides
by the Elbe, barefoot walks
with the girl you liked.

Before I left, we got tattoos together
from a guy doing flash at *Inside Bar* –
a pine on my right calf, a mountain on
your left ribcage. I like to think there's
part of me there in your skin,
nesting by your ribs. The same way I'll look
at my leg-tree and think of the voice
that's unspooling from my phone speaker:
The world is full of lonely people, be brave.

DAWN CONVERSATION

Are you close?

Yes, I hate her and I love her
In Italian we say that love and hate are the same thing,
The line between them is very thin and blurry –
They're both fire.

Skinny Dipping La Gouille de Salin

First, I'm shy, shrinking back. She bites my toes.
They blush bright red. I wade in slow,

kiss the backs of rocks with the palms of my feet.
She licks my knees with an ice tongue.

I plunge into her like falling through a glass ceiling,
her cold sinking through to my bones, every hair rigid

and screaming in symphonic chorus, my nipples
sticking up like tall pines. And I'm on fire

my breath pours out in flames, my throat burnt away,
tingling like a wind chime. I succumb completely

to her: empress of the valley. Pebbles bow
their silky crowns moulded by her touch,

larches straighten their backs on guard. She hisses
around the island of my body, *look how small you are*

and I, through chattering teeth reply
And look how alive.

Acknowledgements

'Painting People', 'Cappuccinos', 'I Want to Stand Naked in the School Hall', 'Dunnock', 'Little Boy on the Train', 'Seagull', 'Meritocracy', 'The Moon Stripping' and 'It's Okay to Break' are published in my pamphlet, *Ugly Bird* (Smith/Doorstop 2021)

'I Want to Stand Naked in the School Hall' was a winner of Foyle Young Poets of the Year competition 2019. It also appears in the anthology *She Will Soar*, edited by Ana Sampson (Pan Macmillan 2020), and in Issue 1 of *PrettyFace* (Holly Bullcock 2020)

'Cappuccinos', 'Meritocracy' and 'Dunnock' appear in issue 65 of *The North* (The Poetry Business, 2020)

'Little Boy on the Train' was shortlisted in Wells Festival of Literature 2020.

This book would not be possible without my incredible mentor and friend, Vicky Morris. Thank you for dedicating so much of your time to help me edit, unpaid. Thank you for our 1am conversations, for supporting me through hard times and always knowing what to say. Thank you for running Hive, an organisation that has given me and many others opportunities we could never have dreamed of; helped build careers and change lives. You are amazing.

Thanks also to Fern Beattie for believing in my work and for founding Write Bloody UK. To Steve Dearden and The Writing Squad, another wonderful organisation that has helped shape my writing career. Thank you to Malika Booker for being an excellent teacher. Thank you to Helen Bowell for your help and guidance. I'm very grateful for the encouragement and support from my teachers and tutors, especially Claire Campion, Sarah Davis, Helen Barr and Sophie Ratcliffe.

Thank You to Céline Marro, for welcoming me into your beautiful family in Tignes, where most of these poems were written.

To Margaret (Mam'am) and Hayden Hollingsworth – *Don't Quit*

To Lesley Smith, Mandy Hardcastle and Chris Hollingsworth.

Thank you Antonia Jameson, Billy Morrissey, Doaa Shabbir, Ebonie Peters, Ethan Gray, Isobel ('Big Sis') Hinchcliffe, Rachelita Mund and Savinay Sood, for being there through my lowest moments, for your kindness, and for being all round wonderful human beings – I love you.

And thank you Mia, for putting up with me.

About the Author

LAUREN HOLLINGSWORTH-SMITH is a poet and artist based in Rotherham and Oxford. She is a member of The Writing Squad and Hive's Poetry Collective. Lauren's work has been published in several anthologies including She Will Soar (Pan Macmillan 2020). Her debut pamphlet *Ugly Bird* won the 2020 New Poets Prize. She won the Foyle Young Poets of the Year award in 2019 and was highly commended in the Young Northern Writers' award. Lauren has performed at various events and festivals, including Ledbury Poetry Festival, Kendal Poetry Festival and Off the Shelf Festival of Words. She studies English and French at Oxford University.

If You Like Lauren Hollingsworth-Smith, Lauren Likes...

The Cardboard Sublime
Oliver Sedano-Jones

What We Are Given
Ollie O' Neill

Ping!
Iain Whiteley

Bloody beautiful poetry books.

Write Bloody UK is an independent poetry publisher passionate
about bringing the voices of UK poets to the masses.
Trailing after Write Bloody Publishing (US) and
Write Bloody North (Canada), we are committed to
handling the creation, distribution and marketing of our authors;
binding their words in beautiful, velvety-to-the-touch books
and touring loudly with them through UK cities.

Support independent authors, artists, and presses.

Want to know more about Write Bloody UK books, authors, and events?
Join our mailing list at

www.writebloodyuk.co.uk

WRITE BLOODY UK BOOKS

www.ingramcontent.com/pod-product-compliance
Lightning Source LLC
Chambersburg PA
CBHW020213090426

42734CB00008B/1048

* 9 7 8 1 8 3 8 0 3 3 2 5 5 *